T0165113

THE BOOK OF

SIMPLE SONGS
& CIRCLES

Wonderful songs and rhymes passed down from generation to generation

Compiled by John M. Feierabend

GIA FIRST STEPS • CHICAGO

It has come to our attention that two songs printed in this collection no longer meet the GIA and FAME standards for use with children. As such, we recommend that parents, caregivers, and teachers no longer use "Possum Up a Gum Tree" (p. 30) and "Jump Jim-a-long" (p. 58). For more information, visit giamusic.com/DEI.

Compiled by
John M. Feierabend

Artwork: Diana Appleton
Design: Nina Fox

GIA First Steps is an imprint of
GIA Publications, Inc.

ISBN: 978-1-57999-057-2
G-4978

Once upon a time, parents (and grandparents) soothed and amused their babies with songs that were sung to them when they were children. As those babies grew up and became parents, they would sing those same tunes to their children. In this way, wonderful songs and rhymes would be passed orally, linking one generation to another through shared memories of comfort and joy. Families are more rushed for time than they ever were, and extended families are much less common than they once were. Because of this, cherished songs and rhymes, many of them hundreds of years old, are gradually being forgotten. Our genuine traditional music is in danger of being supplanted by market-driven ear candy, tunes that may provide a temporary rush but exist mostly to help sell this year's hot new toys.

The *First Steps in Music* series of books and recordings is an attempt to preserve the rich repertoire of traditional and folk literature; to enable today's families to remember and to learn songs and rhymes that have inspired wonder and joy in children for generations.

The material in this book has been gathered over the past twenty years. Many of the most interesting examples, not readily available in print elsewhere, were collected from the elderly who often recalled songs and/or rhymes with great affection, reminding them of loving moments they had shared with young people in the past.

These simple songs are among the easiest to sing for very young children. These simple circle games are among those that are within the capabilities for even the youngest walking children.

It is my hope that the collections of songs and rhymes presented in this series will help parents and other loving adults amuse and inspire wonder in children, for generations to come.

John M. Feierabend

How to Sing Simple Songs

Just as baby should hear a wide range of vocabulary and will make early attempts at the easy-to-speak words, these simplest of songs should be a part of the songs baby hears to provide some examples that will be easy for baby to sing when his/her singing begins. These songs have a limited melodic range and will likely be among the first songs he/she will attempt to sing.

sing to child

children sing to each other

child sings alone

Before age two, baby should not be expected to sing (although some do); rather, these songs are sung at this age so baby can become familiar with some songs that will be easily accessible when baby makes his/her first singing attempts.

These songs are presented in the keys of F and G to encourage a pleasant, light singing voice. For some, these songs may feel a little high but by singing lightly, these keys will prepare baby to eventually have the best use of his/her correct singing voice. As toddlers become familiar with the songs, you may try leaving off the last word of the song or of a phrase to see if baby will fill in the blank. When this happens, the singing of the whole song will not be far behind.

SIMPLE SONGS

Au Clair de la Lune/Pierrot
(In the Evening Moonlight) *French*

Au Clair de la Lu - ne, Mon a - mi Pier - rot,
In the eve - ning moon - light stands Pierr-ot to - night.

Prè - tes - moi ta plu - me Pour é - crire un mot.
Plead-ing for a pen-cil so that he may write.

Verse

Au Clair de la Lune,
Mon ami Pierrot,
Prètes-moi ta plume
Pour écrire un mot.

Translation:

In the evening moonlight
    stands Pierrot tonight.
Pleading for a pencil so that
    he may write.

Babylon's Fallin'

Ba - by - lon's fall - in', fall - in', fall - in',

Ba - by - lon's fall - in' to rise no more.

Verse

Babylon's fallin', fallin', fallin',
Babylon's fallin' to rise no more.

Bounce High

Bounce   high,   Bounce   low,

Bounce   the   ball   to   Shi - loh.

Verse

Bounce high,
Bounce low,
Bounce the ball to Shiloh.

Bye, Baby Bunting

Bye,   ba - by bunt - ing.   Dad - dy's   gone   a

hunt - ing,   To   catch   a   lit - tle   rab - bit skin   To

wrap   his   ba - by   bunt - ing   in.

Verse

Bye, baby bunting.
Daddy's gone a hunting,
To catch a little rabbit skin
To wrap his baby bunting in.

Did You Ever, Ever, Ever

Did you ev - er, ev - er, ev - er, in your

long leg - ged life, See a long leg - ged

sail - or and his long leg - ged wife?

Verse 1

Did you ever, ever, ever, in your
long legged life,
See a long legged sailor and his
long legged wife?

Verse 2

No, I never, never, never, in my
long legged life,
Saw a long legged sailor and his
long legged wife.

Verse 3

Did you ever…short legged…

Verse 4

No I never…short legged…

Verses 5 and 6

…bow legged…

Verses 7 and 8

…one legged…

Verses 9 and 10

…no legged…

Fais Dodo *Cajun*

Fais do - do, Co - las mon p'tit frè - re,
Fais do - do, and let us go dream - ing,

Fais do - do, t'au - ras du lo - lo.
Fais do - do, come dream - ing with me.

Verse

Fais dodo, Colas mon p'tit frère,
Fais dodo, t'auras du lolo.

Translation:

Fais dodo, and let us go dreaming,
Fais dodo, come dreaming with me.

Frog in the Meadow

Frog in the mead - ow, Can't get him out.

Take a lit - tle stick And stir him a - bout.

Verse

Frog in the meadow,
Can't get him out.
Take a little stick
And stir him about.

Go 'Round the Mountain

Go 'round the moun-tain, To - di did-dle-dum,

to - di did-dle-dum, Go 'round the moun-tain,

To - di did - dle - dum dee.

Verse 1

Go 'round the mountain,
Todi diddledum, todi diddledum,
Go 'round the mountain,
Todi diddledum dee.

Verse 2

Show me your finger,
Todi diddledum, todi diddledum…

Verse 3

Select your partner,
Todi diddledum, todi diddledum…

*during the first verse, walk randomly
   around the room*
*during the second verse, choose a partner by
   stopping near a child and shaking a finger
   at him/her*
*during the third verse, the partners walk
   around the room, holding hands*
*at the end of the song, repeat from the
   beginning while the children search for
   new partners*

Good News! Chariot's Comin'

Good news! Char - iot's com - in',

Good news! Char - iot's com - in',

Good news! Char - iot's com - in' and I

don't want you to leave - a me be - hind.

Verse

Good news! Chariot's comin',
Good news! Chariot's comin',
Good news! Chariot's comin' and I
  don't want you to leave-a me behind.

Grandma Grunts

Grand - ma Grunts said a cur - i - ous thing,

"Boys can whis - tle but girls must sing."

Verse 1

Grandma Grunts said a curious thing,
"Boys can whistle but girls must sing."

Verse 2

That is what I heard her say,
'Twas no longer than yesterday.

Hop Old Squirrel

Hop   old   squirrel,   Ei - del - dum,   ei - del - dum.

Hop   old   squirrel,   Ei - del - dum - dee.

Hop   old   squirrel,   Ei - del - dum,   ei - del - dum.

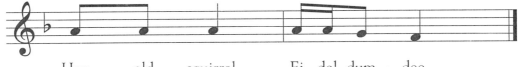

Hop   old   squirrel,   Ei - del - dum - dee.

Verse

Hop old squirrel,
Ei-del-dum, ei-del-dum.
Hop old squirrel, Ei-del-dum-dee.
Hop old squirrel,
Ei-del-dum, ei-del-dum.
Hop old squirrel, Ei-del-dum-dee.

Hot Cross Buns

Hot   cross   buns,   Hot   cross   buns.

One   a   pen - ny,   two   a   pen - ny,   Hot   cross   buns.

Verse 1

Hot cross buns,
Hot cross buns.
One a penny, two a penny,
Hot cross buns.

Verse 2

If you have no daughters,
Give them to your sons.
One a penny, two a penny,
Hot cross buns.

I Have Lost My Closet Key

I have lost my clos - et key

In my la - dy's gar - den.

I have lost my clos - et key

In my la - dy's gar - den.

Verse 1

I have lost my closet key
In my lady's garden.
I have lost my closet key
In my lady's garden.

Verse 2

I have found my closet key
In my lady's garden.
I have found my closet key
In my lady's garden.

Dutch Girl

I'm a lit-tle Dutch girl, Dutch girl, Dutch girl.

I'm a lit-tle Dutch girl, Far a-cross the sea.

Verse 1

I'm a little Dutch girl,
Dutch girl, Dutch girl.
I'm a little Dutch girl,
Far across the sea.

Verse 2

I'm a little Dutch boy…

Verse 3

Go away, I hate you…

Verse 4

Why do you hate me?…

Verse 5

Because you stole my necklace…

Verse 6

What color was it?…

Verse 7

It was gold…

Verse 8

Here is your necklace…

Verse 9

Now we're getting married…

I'm Trampin'

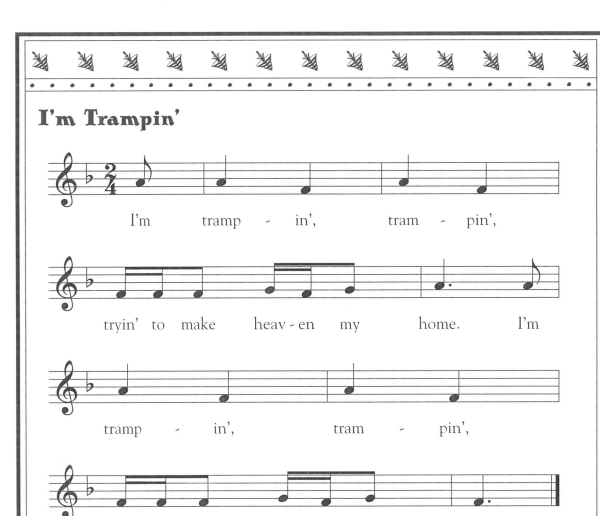

I'm tramp - in', tram - pin',

tryin' to make heav - en my home. I'm

tramp - in', tram - pin',

tryin' to make heav - en my home.

Verse

I'm trampin', trampin',
  tryin' to make heaven my home.
I'm trampin', trampin',
  tryin' to make heaven my home.

It's Raining, It's Pouring

It's rain - ing, it's pour - ing, The old man is snor - ing. Bumped his head and he went to bed And he could - n't get up in the morn - ing.

Verse

It's raining, it's pouring,
The old man is snoring.
Bumped his head and he went to bed
And he couldn't get up in the morning.

Johnny Had One Friend

John-ny had one friend, One friend, one friend.

John-ny had one friend, John-ny had two.

Verse

Johnny had one friend,
One friend, one friend.
Johnny had one friend,
Johnny had two.

tap with said number of fingers on leg
repeat until "Johnny had five friends"

Mother, May I Go Out to Swim?

Moth - er, may I go out to swim?

Yes, my dar - ling daugh - ter.

Hang your clothes on the hick - o - ry limb, But

don't go near the wa - ter.

Verse

Mother, may I go out to swim?
Yes, my darling daughter.
Hang your clothes on the hickory limb,
But don't go near the water.

The Boatmen

Oh, the boat-men dance, the boat-men sing. The

boat-men up to ev'-ry-thing. And when the boat-men

get to shore, They spend their cash and work for more.

Verse

Oh, the boatmen dance, the boatmen sing.
The boatmen up to ev'rything.
And when the boatmen get to shore,
They spend their cash and work for more.

Oliver Twist

O - li - ver Twist, you can't do this, So

what's the use of try - ing?

Touch your knees, touch your toes,

Clap your hands and a - round you go.

Verse

Oliver Twist, you can't do this,
So what's the use of trying?
Touch your knees, touch your toes,
Clap your hands and around you go.

perform motions as indicated

Peep Squirrel

Peep squir - rel, peep squir - rel,

Do - da, did - dle - um, do - da, did - dle - um,

Peep squir - rel, peep squir - rel,

Do - da, did - dle - um, dum.

Verse

Peep squirrel, peep squirrel,
Do-da, diddle-um, do-da, diddle-um,
Peep squirrel, peep squirrel,
Do-da, diddle-um, dum.

Pitter, Patter

Pit-ter, pat-ter, pit-ter, pat-ter, Lis-ten to the rain.

Pit-ter, pat-ter, pit-ter, pat-ter, On my win-dow pane.

Verse

Pitter, patter, pitter, patter,
Listen to the rain.
Pitter, patter, pitter, patter,
On my window pane.

Rain, Rain, Go Away

Rain,   rain,   go   a - way.

Come a - gain some   oth - er   day.

Verse

Rain, rain, go away.
Come again some other day.

'Round and 'Round

'Round and 'round the wheel goes 'round.

As it turns the corn is ground.

Verse

'Round and 'round the wheel goes 'round.
As it turns the corn is ground.

'Possum Up the Gum Tree

'Pos-sum up the gum tree, Coon is in the hol-low,

Lit - tle girl at our house, She can real - ly wal -ler.

Verse

'Possum up the gum tree,
Coon is in the hollow,
Little girl at our house,
She can really waller.

Riding in a Buggy

Rid-ing in a bug-gy Miss Ma - ry Jane, Miss

Ma - ry Jane, Miss Ma - ry Jane.

Rid-ing in a bug-gy Miss Ma - ry Jane, I'm a

long ways from home.

Verse

Riding in a buggy Miss Mary Jane,
Miss Mary Jane, Miss Mary Jane.
Riding in a buggy Miss Mary Jane,
I'm a long ways from home.

Rock-a-Bye

Rock - a - bye,   Rock - a - bye   a   ba - by.

Rock - a - bye,   Rock - a - bye,

Rock - a - bye   a   ba - by.

Verse

Rock-a-bye,
Rock-a-bye a baby.
Rock-a-bye,
Rock-a-bye,
Rock-a-bye a baby.

Seesaw, Margery Daw

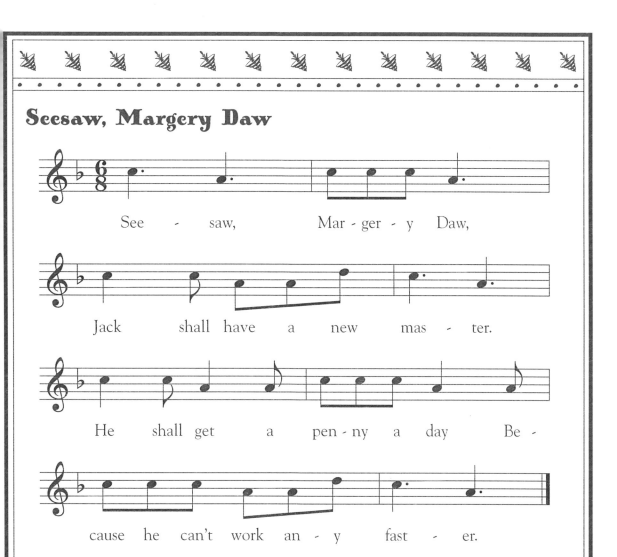

See - saw, Mar - ger - y Daw,

Jack shall have a new mas - ter.

He shall get a pen - ny a day Be -

cause he can't work an - y fast - er.

Verse

Seesaw, Margery Daw,
Jack shall have a new master.
He shall get a penny a day
Because he can't work any faster.

Sailor, Sailor

Sail - or, sail - or on the sea,

Sail - or, sail - or on the sea,

Sail - or, sail - or on the sea, What

trea - sures have you brought for me?

Verse 1

Sailor, sailor on the sea,
Sailor, sailor on the sea,
Sailor, sailor on the sea,
What treasures have you brought for me?

Verse 2

Farmer, farmer on the land…
I've gold and jewels in my hand.

Verse 3

You have missed the number plain…
So I shall sail the seas again.
or
You have guessed the number true…
Now you may sail the ocean blue.

one child stands behind the other child; the child in front (the farmer) sings the first verse; the child in back (the sailor) sings the second verse and holds up one to five fingers; the farmer tries to guess that number; if the guess is wrong, the sailor sings "You have missed," and the farmer selects another child to be the farmer; if the guess is right, the sailor sings, "You have guessed," and the farmer becomes the new sailor, and the old sailor picks a new farmer

the book of simple songs & circles

Shosheen Sho *Scottish*

Sho - sheen Sho,   Ba - by boy,   Fa - ther's pride,   Moth - er's joy.

Bird - ie sleeps   in the nest,   Sun doth sink   in the west.

Verse

Shosheen Sho, Baby boy,
Father's pride, Mother's joy.
Birdie sleeps in the nest,
Sun doth sink in the west.

Tattle Tail

Tat - tle tail, tat - tle tail,

Hang your britch - es on a nail.

Hang 'em high, hang 'em low,

Hang 'em at the pic - ture show.

Verse

Tattle tail, tattle tail,
Hang your britches on a nail.
Hang 'em high, hang 'em low,
Hang 'em at the picture show.

Trick or Treat

Trick or treat, smell my feet.

Give me some-thing good to eat.

Verse

Trick or treat, smell my feet.
Give me something good to eat.

There She Goes

There   she goes,   There   she goes,

All   dressed up   in   her   Sun - day   clothes.

Verse

There she goes,
There she goes,
All dressed up in
    her Sunday clothes.

Ball Rolling...

use the following ball rolling songs to roll the ball to baby and have baby roll the ball back to you; each ball roll should coincide with a phrase of the song

Cuckoo, Cherry Tree

BALL ROLLING

Cuck - oo,   Cher-ry   tree,   Catch the

ball,   Roll   it   to   me.

Verse
Cuckoo,
Cherry tree,
Catch the ball,
Roll it to me.

I Roll the Ball

BALL ROLLING

I roll the ball to ba - by, she rolls it back to me. I roll the ball to ba - by, she rolls it back to me. Roll the ball, roll the ball, Roll the ball, roll the ball, I roll the ball to ba - by, she rolls it back to me.

Verse

I roll the ball to <u>baby</u>,
  she rolls it back to me.
I roll the ball to <u>baby</u>,
  she rolls it back to me.

Roll the ball, roll the ball,
Roll the ball, roll the ball,
I roll the ball to <u>baby</u>,
  she rolls it back to me.

substitute baby's name

En Roulant (On, Roll On) *French*

BALL ROLLING

En rou - lant, Ma bou - le rou - lant,
On, roll on, My ball roll on.

En rou - lant, Ma bou - le.
On, roll on, My ball roll on.

Verse

En roulant,
Ma boule roulant,
En roulant,
Ma boule.

Translation:

On, roll on,
My ball roll on.
On, roll on,
My ball roll on.

Down by the Greenwood

One day I was sit-ting in my fath-er's hall, I

saw three babes a - play - ing ball. All day long and I

love you all, Down by the green-wood sid - e-o.

Verse

One day I was sitting in my
   father's hall,
I saw three babes a-playing ball.
All day long and I love you all,
Down by the greenwood sid-e-o.

Roll, Catch

Roll, catch, roll, catch, Roll, catch the ball.

Roll, catch, roll, catch, Roll, catch the ball.

Verse

Roll, catch, roll, catch,
Roll, catch the ball.
Roll, catch, roll, catch,
Roll, catch the ball.

Roll that Round Ball

BALL ROLLING

Roll that round ball down to town,

Roll that round ball down to town,

Roll that round ball down to town,

Roll that round ball down to town.

Verse

Roll that round ball down to town,
Roll that round ball down to town,
Roll that round ball down to town,
Roll that round ball down to town.

Sweet Water Rolling

Sweet wa - ter roll - ing, Sweet wa - ter roll,

Roll - ing from the foun - tain, Sweet wa - ter roll.

Verse

Sweet water rolling,
Sweet water roll,
Rolling from the fountain,
Sweet water roll.

CIRCLES

How to Sing Circles

These circle games are among the first ones that a toddler can participant in. Most of these games require little more than walking around in a circle with a "surprise" ending. The excitement builds for baby as the song progresses to the climactic moment where the

walk behind child

walk side by side

walk facing each other

anticipated motion occurs. Some of the circle games also include a rhyme to chant which ends with all jumping back up ready to repeat the games again and again. Hopefully these circle games will be the first steps to a lifetime of sharing music and movement with family and friends.

at this age, circles are best played with the parent and toddler walking around in a circle side by side or with the parent walking behind the toddler if he/she needs some added support

Walking around in one large circle while all hold hands is physically uncomfortable for toddlers. While holding hands in a large circle, the toddler will find it difficult to twist his or her body to successfully walk forward in the circle. Rather, children should walk around in the circle without holding each other's hands and instead follow each other in a line around in a circle.

Allee Galloo

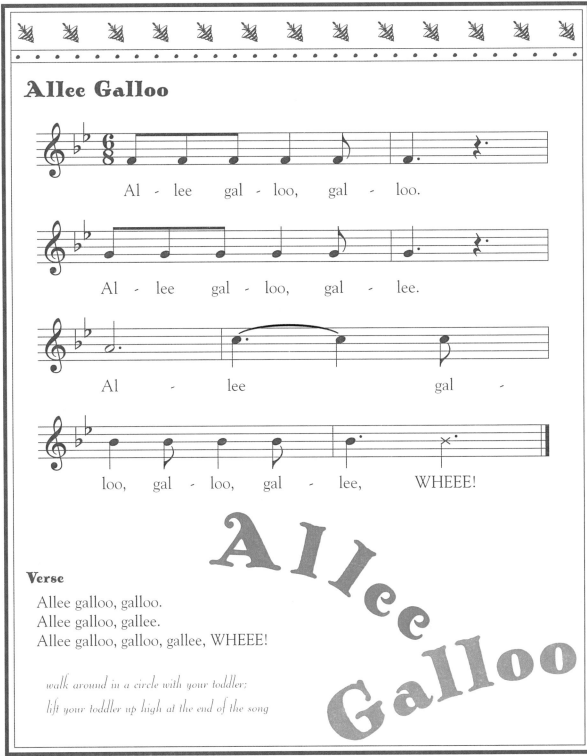

Al - lee gal - loo, gal - loo.

Al - lee gal - loo, gal - lee.

Al - lee gal - loo, gal -

loo, gal - loo, gal - lee, WHEEE!

Verse

Allee galloo, galloo.
Allee galloo, gallee.
Allee galloo, galloo, gallee, WHEEE!

walk around in a circle with your toddler;
lift your toddler up high at the end of the song

the book of simple songs & circles

Come on Boys

Come on boys and hush your talk - ing,

All join hands and let's go walk - ing,

Walk a - long John, with your pa - per col - lar on,

Walk a - long John, with your pa - per col - lar on.

Verse

Come on boys and hush your talking,
All join hands and let's go walking,
Walk along John, with your paper
   collar on,
Walk along John, with your paper
   collar on.

*one person is the leader and takes the group for
a walk winding around the room*

Down in the Valley

Down in the val - ley two by two, Oh ba - by,

two by two, Oh ba - by, two by two.

Down in the val - ley two by two,

Rise, su - gar, rise.

the book of simple songs & circles

Verse 1

Down in the valley two by two,
Oh baby, two by two,
Oh baby, two by two.
Down in the valley two by two,
Rise, sugar, rise.

Verse 2

Let me see you make a motion,
two by two…

Verse 3

Choose another partner, two by two…

*begin with an odd number of children; all
children find a partner; the last child goes to
the center of the circle*

during verse 1, the children walk around in pairs

*during verse 2, the child in the middle shows a
motion; the other children imitate that motion*

*during verse 3 (for younger children), they
scatter around, find a new partner and rejoin
the circle; the remaining child goes to the
center*

*during verse 3 (for older children), the outside
circle goes in one direction and the inside circle
goes in the opposite direction; the child in the
middle joins the inside circle*

*at the end of the song, all stop and grab a
partner; the remaining child goes to the middle*

Giro, Giro, Tondo (Ring a Ring a Round-o) *Italian*

Gi-ro, gi-ro, ton-do, Il pa-ne sot-to il for-no, Un
Ring a ring a round-o, The bread is bak-ing brown-o. A

maz-zo di vi-o-le, Le do-no a chi le vuo-le; Le
bunch of vio-lets pick them To give to the one who wants them. We'll

vuo-le la San-dri-na, E cas-chi la piú pic-ci-na.
give them to the tall-est And down falls the one that's small-est.

Verse

Giro, giro, tondo,
Il pane sotto il forno,
Un mazzo di viole,
Le dono a chi le vuole;
Le vuole la Sandrina,
E caschi la piú piccina.

*walk around in a circle, and "fall down" at the
end of the song*

Translation:

Ring a ring a round-o,
The bread is baking brown-o.
A bunch of violets pick them
To give to the one who wants
them.
We'll give them to the tallest
And down falls the one that's
smallest.

Santa Maloney

Here we go San - ta Ma - lo - ney,

Here we go San - ta Ma - lo - ney,

Here we go San - ta Ma - lo - ney as

we go 'round a - bout.

Verse

Here we go Santa Maloney,
Here we go Santa Maloney,
Here we go Santa Maloney
as we go 'round about.

*walk around in a circle for this verse; make up
other verses with actions that can be performed
while walking around in a circle such as:*

tap your hands on your legs... or

put your hands on your head...

The Mulberry Bush

Here we go 'round the Mul - ber - ry bush,

Mul - ber - ry bush, Mul - ber - ry bush.

Here we go 'round the Mul - ber - ry bush So

ear - ly in the morn - ing.

Verse 1

Here we go 'round the Mulberry bush,
Mulberry bush, Mulberry bush.
Here we go 'round the Mulberry bush
So early in the morning.

Verse 2

This is the way we wash our clothes...

Verse 3

This is the way we wring out our clothes...

Verse 4

This is the way we hang up our clothes...

Verse 5

This is the way we iron our clothes...

Verse 6

This is the way we fold our clothes...

*walk around in a circle during the first verse;
during the other verses, pantomine the motions
suggested; have children make up other verses*

Jump, Jim-a-long

Jump, Jim - a - long, Jim - a - long, Jo - sie,

Jump, Jim - a - long, Jim - a - long, Joe.

Jump, Jim - a - long, Jim - a - long, Jo - sie,

Jump, Jim - a - long, Jim - a - long, Joe.

Verse

Jump, Jim-a-long, Jim-a-long, Josie,
Jump, Jim-a-long, Jim-a-long, Joe.
Jump, Jim-a-long, Jim-a-long, Josie,
Jump, Jim-a-long, Jim-a-long, Joe.

jump around in a circle; repeat the song many times choosing different ways to move around the circle (for example, walking, hopping, skipping, etc.)

Little Red Caboose

Lit-tle red ca-boose,   lit-tle red   ca-boose,

Lit-tle red   ca-boose be-hind the   train.   Toot, toot,

Smoke-stack on its   back,   rol-lin' down the   track,

Lit-tle red   ca-boose be-hind the   train.   Toot, toot.

Verse

Little red caboose, little red caboose,
Little red caboose behind the train.
  Toot, toot,
Smokestack on its back, rollin' down
  the track,
Little red caboose behind the train.
  Toot, toot.

this is a follow-the-leader game; one toddler leads the others around the room; with each repeat, pick a new leader

Little Sally Walker

Lit-tle Sal-ly Walk-er, sit-ting in a sau-cer; Rise, Sal-ly,

rise, wipe a - way your eyes. Turn to the east and

turn to the west And turn to the one that you like the best.

Verse

Little Sally Walker, sitting in a saucer;
Rise, Sally, rise, wipe away your eyes.
Turn to the east and turn to the west
And turn to the one that you like the
  best.

*children stand in a circle while one child sits in
  the center; as the song is sung, the child in the
  center pantomimes the phrases "rise" and "wipe
  your eyes"
during the last two lines of the song, the child in
  the center covers his/her eyes with one hand
  and points with the other hand while turning
  around at the end of the song, the child being
  pointed to is the next "Sally"*

No Bears Out Tonight

No bears out to-night, No bears out to-night,

No bears out to-night, They've all gone a-way.

Verse

No bears out tonight,
No bears out tonight,
No bears out tonight,
They've all gone away.

walk around in a circle and squat
down at the end of the song

Ring Around the Rosey

Ring a-round the rose-y, A pock-et full of pos-ies. Ash-es, ash-es, we all fall down!

Verse

Ring around the rosey,
A pocket full of posies.
Ashes, ashes, we all fall down!

walk around in a circle, and "fall down" at the end of the song

Ring-o, Ring-o, Rang-o

Ring - o, Ring - o, Rang - o, See the child - ren

three - o, Sit - ting by the li - lac bush,

All to - geth - er, hush, hush, hush.

Verse

Ring-o, Ring-o, Rang-o,
See the children three-o,
Sitting by the lilac bush,
All together, hush, hush, hush.

with one child in the middle, children walk around in a circle and squat down at the end and close their eyes; the child in the center chooses another child and trades places; the new child in the center chants, "Come out, come out wherever you are" then the children in the circle open their eyes and repeat the game

Sally Go 'Round the Sun

Sal-ly go 'round the sun, Sal-ly go 'round the

moon, Sal - ly go 'round the

chim - ney pot, Ev - 'ry af - ter - noon. BOOM!

Verse

Sally go 'round the sun,
Sally go 'round the moon,
Sally go 'round the chimney pot,
Ev'ry afternoon.
BOOM!

walk around in a circle with your toddler;
lift your toddler up high at the end of the song

Snail, Snail

Snail,   snail,   snail,   snail,

Go   a - round   and   'round   and   'round.

Verse

Snail, snail, snail, snail,
Go around and 'round and 'round.

children hold hands in a circle; one person designated as the leader takes the line on an inward spiral; when well-wound, the leader takes the line on an outward spiral traveling between the rows of children still on the inward spiral; when finished, the circle will be facing out; perform another inward and outward spiral to bring the children back to facing into the center

Take Your Feet

Take your feet out the sand,

Take your feet out the sand,

Take your feet out the sand and

stick 'em in the mud!

Verse

Take your feet out the sand,
Take your feet out the sand,
Take your feet out the sand and
  stick 'em in the mud!

Other examples:
Take your feet out the snow...
Take your feet out the jello...
Take your feet out the cement...

travel around the room as if lifting feet out of sand;

create additional verses and motions by changing the word "sand"

The Leaves Are Green, the Nuts Are Brown

The leaves are green, the nuts are brown. They

hang so high they won't come down.

Leave them a - lone 'til frost - y weath-er And

they will all - fall down to - geth - er.

Verse

The leaves are green, the nuts are brown.
They hang so high they won't come down.
Leave them alone 'til frosty weather
And they will all fall down together.

walk around in a circle, and squat
down at the end of the song

Three Times Around

Three times a-round went our gal-lant ship, And

three times a-round went she.

Three times a-round went our gal-lant ship, And we

sank to the bot-tom of the sea.

Verse

Three times around went our gallant ship,
And three times around went she.
Three times around went our gallant ship,
And we sank to the bottom of the sea.

walk around in a circle with your toddler; during the last
phrase, sink down to the ground and chant the following
rhyme while tapping on the floor:

(Spoken)

Penny on the water,
Penny on the sea.
Up jumps a little fish
And up jumps me!

jump up and play the circle game again

Walk Daniel

Walk Dan - iel, walk Dan - iel. Walk Dan - iel,

walk Dan - iel. The oth - er way, Dan - iel.

The oth - er way, Dan - iel.

Verse

Walk Daniel, walk Daniel.
Walk Daniel, walk Daniel.
The other way, Daniel.
The other way, Daniel.

walk around in a circle; during the second half of the song, change directions and walk the other way; substitute other children's names, and create other ways of moving around the room

Index